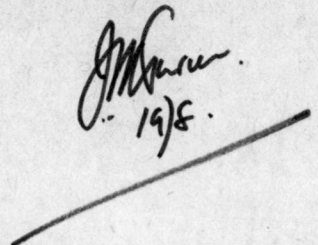

# THE WORD IS THE SEED

George Appleton

# THE WORD IS THE SEED

*Meditations Starting from the Bible*

London
SPCK

First published 1976
SPCK
Holy Trinity Church
Marylebone Road
London NW1 4DU

Printed in Great Britain by
Bocardo & Church Army Press Ltd,
Cowley, Oxford

ISBN 0 281 02909 1

# CONTENTS

# FOREWORD BY SIR JOHN BETJEMAN

These prayers of George Appleton suit me
well which is why I warmly commend them
in this preface.

Willing to pray, the mind waits on the
edge of a sliding stream. The prayers push
the boat off out into the current. Once in
the stream, the prayer is effortless com-
pulsion carrying the mind along and sometimes swerving close to the presence of
the Creator.

The short lines and the way they are
printed on the page carry me along at the
right pace. They make skipping impossible.
They may be used in omnibuses and trains
and even in airports. One at a time is
enough. And time disappears under their
benevolent, under their invigorating influ-
ence. They can even make one smile as in
Poor Aaron, page 7.

*John Betjeman*

# SEED AND WORD
Mark 4.14   Luke 8.11, 15

O God,
   it is good to know
   that there is a Sower
   who brings the seed.
   I have only to prepare the soil
   for the seed he brings —
   an honest and good heart.
Give me that heart, O God.

O Divine Sower,
   the seed must find entry
   through each day's routine,
   guarded in the traffic of life,
   the babel of other voices,
   the distractions of other wills,
   the presence of other views,
   a quiet and listening heart.
Give me that heart, O God.

O Divine Sower,
   the seed must have depth,
   firmly rooted against wind and storm,
   nourished in heat or dryness,
   preserved in frost and cold,
   drawing its nourishment
   from the depths of being.
Give me such a heart, O God.

O Divine Sower,
    the seed must have room
    even with other good seeds
    of my own choosing,
    let alone from weeds and nettles,
    leisure for quiet thought and growth
    and a quiet heart of faith.
Give me such a heart, O God.

O Divine Sower,
    at its right time the seed will germinate,
    the thin young blade will push its way
    through the heart's soil,
    the ear will bud and fill,
    the flower will open its face of beauty
    at the moment of maturity.
Give me a patient heart, O God.

O Divine Sower,
    my ear is attent and listening —
    a sound of gentle stillness,
    a still small voice,
    at times a clap of thunder to warn,
    a lightning flash to illumine.
    Give me a listening heart,
    O dear my God,
to the Seed of thy Word.

# I AM

Exodus 3.15

That is all that you can say of me
    unconceptualizable,
    unverbalizable.
Yet the source of being,
    the creator of all,
    the ground of existence,
    ultimate reality.
Unconditional
    ever unchanging,
    ever at rest,
    yet always proceeding forth.
I AM what I always am,
    I AM what I shall always be,
    I was, I am, I will be
The source of your being,
    the content of your life,
    the goal of your future,
As I was in the beginning,
    am now in this moment of time,
        and ever shall be.
You too my child
    can say 'I am'
        because you derive from me.
You can resist, my child,
    You can rebel,
    ignore, avoid the amness
        I have given you.

But down eternity
   through time and space,
   through the kingdom of the dead
   and temptations of hell
You may move in drift or flight
   but never escape from
      omnipresent
      eternal
      deathless love.

# BEING

Exodus 3.14

O Thou who art Being,
out of the depth of my being
I stretch up to thine.

For thou art eternal,
thou art perfect,
thou art limitless.

I am a child of time,
unperfected as yet,
confined within my limitations.

As yet immature,
as always falling short,
self-imprisoning.

Yet as the germ of life
cracks the shell of the seed
and strains towards the light

So I, from the seed divinely given,
reach upwards towards thee,
drawn by the likeness.

I too am being,
being of thy Being,
atman of thy Atman.

Drawn by limitless Love
which thou dost give,
making me part of thee,

I too am love
stretching upward
to my source in thee.

And to right and left
before and behind and in and around
to others.

Let me go down,
deep down within,
until I find
the spring of being,
the well of love.

## POOR AARON
Exodus 32.23

They wanted a god they could see
   like the other nations
   to go before them in battle,
   to be a symbol.
Their leader had disappeared
   on the mountain
   and Aaron was weak, only a mouthpiece,
   not yet priest of the tabernacle.
So they brought their jewels
   and there came out
   a golden calf,
Not a gentle calf
   for sacrifice
   but a bull of strength
   like the Assyrian gods.
And up on the mountain
   Moses conferring with God
   had heard the command —
      Thou shalt make no graven image
      nor the likeness
      of anything
      in heaven or earth.
For God is spirit,
   in being unoriginate,
   Creator and Mover
   of all that lives,
   eternal, unchanging,
   bearing his people,

not carried by them.
And there was Aaron
    making an image
    of the invisible God.
        Poor Aaron!

# THE HOLY OF HOLIES

Hebrews 9.3-5

No image, no likeness of God,
only the tables of the law,
the pot of manna,
Aaron's rod that flowered.

The memories of past mercies,
past wonders,
past forgiveness,
and the righteous will.

And the mercy seat,
the sprinkled blood,
pleading forgiveness.

And the Cherubim,
symbolizing divine presence
not only there,
but there as elsewhere.

A thousand years later
the rent curtain
when flesh and spirit
were torn asunder
in a death
of perfect obedience.

The way is open
to the holiest

and the holiest
released for all.

What the sacrifices of blood
had failed to do
has been accomplished
by the sacrifice of love.

A presence that fills the Universe,
that penetrates every corner,
every prison cell,
every lonely room.

Wherever the spirit of man
is awake and receptive
though often unrecognized,
waiting for welcome.

No image until now,
but at last a likeness
of the divine eternal
incarnated in human life.

And enabling a chain
of endless incarnations.

# COMPANION IN THE FIRE

Daniel 3.25    Isaiah 43.2

Lord, I do not know
   if three men ever went
   through physical fire
   unscathed.
But the message is clear —
   there is always a fourth
   with men in their fire,
   a man such as us
   but bearing thy nature,
   sharing thy eternity.
The promise is clear —
   When thou goest through the waters
      they shall not o'erwhelm thee,
   or through the fire
      it shall not consume or destroy.
To see the fourth
   is safety and salvation,
   the containment of pain,
   its cleansing power,
   the calming of fear.
Lord God,
   let me see the fourth,
   let all men become aware
   that he is present
   if unperceived.
And we shall come through
   unscathed
   nay, cleansed and enriched.

The fire is thine
   and that which is eternal
   shall be preserved,
   indestructible and refined,
   in its predestined beauty and usefulness.

# GUIDING OMNISCIENCE

Exodus 3.13-14

'I will guide thee with my eye',
    my all-seeing eye,
  that sees the foolishness
    and selfishness of men,
    their fears and hopes,
  that sees into thy inner being
    and knows what by my grace
    thou canst become,
  that sees the state of things
    the progress towards my will
    and my world,
  that sees the obstacles
    and the time-lag,
  that sees into the future
    the way the world is going,
    the consequence of present deeds.
I will guide thee with my eye,
    my all-seeing eye,
  that knows what needs to be done
    and what can be said.
  If thou art guide-able,
  if thou art biddable,
I can guide thee with my eye.

# ANGRY ANGUISH

2 Kings 4.27


'Let her alone
   for she is in bitter distress
   and the Lord has hidden it from me
   and has not told me.'
Grant, O God, that I may be
   as perceptive as the prophet,
   as understanding in the sight of bitter anguish,
   as free from defensive retort
   or self-justifying argument.
Let me wait till the anguish has been poured out
   and the bitterness released.
Then let me reply
   with understanding and love,
   with healing and helpfulness,
Speaking a comforting word from you,
   realizing that people
   are wanting light,
   that their angry anguish
   is a cry for meaning,
   an appeal for love.
So let me see into the hearts of men
   and open my heart
   to your heart
      for them.

# SHARP-POINTED
Hebrews 4.12


I know when the word is from thee,
    For it is sharp, two-edged,
    Cutting through all pretence
        to the very core of being,
    Touching the sore spot,
        the hidden selfishness,
        the unacknowledged fear,
    As to the prophet in the Sinai desert
        Not in whirlwind
        or earthquake
        or fire
    But in the still small voice,
    the sound of gentle stillness
    in the depth of the heart.
I shall know
    when the word comes.

# IN THE HEART
Psalm 14.1

The fool says in his heart
   'There is no God.'
Today, O Lord,
   it is the other way round.
The world says that we believers
   are naive and foolish
   to believe in thee.
Lord, we have experienced thee,
   felt thy love,
   sought thy guidance,
   accepted thy grace,
   heard thee speak
   within our being.
There are times, O Lord,
   when faith is tested
   and we have nothing
   to hold on to
   except faith.
Keep the eye of my faith
   undimmed and clear,
that I may see thee
   who art invisible,
and quietly imperturbable
   wait on thee,
   wait for thee,
   wait before thee, dear God.

# MEMORY

Into the computer of my memory
    I insert a word, a thought, a name.
    Immediately
    the silent wheels whirl
    and I remember
    past names, past happenings,
    stored ready
    for the associating key,
    unrecalled for years,
    reviving the past,
    conversing with those from the past,
    resurrecting the dead
    as if present.
Perhaps they are always present,
    just waiting
    the recalling memory,
    the remembered presence.
So now I can speak
    words of welcome and love,
    of gratitude and inquiry,
    words of pardon or apology,
    setting right the past
    in total recall,
    making the bygone past
    into the timeless present.

# DIMINISHING POWERS

Isaiah 46.4

O God, as I grow old
   I am conscious of my mortality,
   I am afraid to go into the unknown,
   I dread the tearing apart
      of soul and body.
   I fear to become a burden
      to loved ones.
But you have said,
   'I have made
   and I will bear
   even to grey hairs!'
The only answer
   to my mortality
   lies in your eternity,
   as my powers diminish
   to be hollowed out,
   ready to be filled
      with your endless life,
O God, as I grow old,
   ready for my last birth.

# NO BETTER THAN MY FATHERS

1 Kings 19.4

I thought, O Lord,
    that I was so much wiser,
    so much more effective,
    understanding the contemporary mood,
    a man for the future.

But now, O Lord,
    at the end of the day
    things are much the same,
    men don't change much
    except perhaps a new mood,
    a new fashion,
    fresh slogans.

Each generation insists
    that it learns the old lessons,
    takes nothing on trust.

Have I, O Lord,
    been as faithful as my fathers,
    as sensitive to the inner word
    regardless of success or failure,
    caring only for integrity
    and obedience?

And what, O Lord,
    about my sons, those who follow me?

19

They seem confident and brash
    with not much regard
    for the man on the way out.

Will they come
    to the same conclusion,
    the same sense of failure
    and also the same humility,
    the same faith?

Will they see
    that though men pass with little done
    and the world remains much the same
Yet the Word of the Lord remains the same,
    his kindnesses never fail,
    his purpose unchanged,
    moving ruthlessly, lovingly
        towards its goal.

Now, O Lord,
    let thy servant
        depart in peace
    for mine eyes have seen
        continuing salvation.

Accept the little I have done
and the much still to be done.
    Let there be a little glory
    and a little candle-flame
        of light and love
        left behind
        for thee from men.

20

# CUTTING EDGE

Luke 6.26

'Woe to you
    when all men speak well
        of you.'

Lord, there doesn't seem much fear
    of this so far.
But I get the message:
    My speech must be seasoned with salt,
    I must speak the truth in love
    but speak it nevertheless
    lest speech should lose
        the point of truth,
        its cutting edge,
    and I become a yes-man
    speaking only what men
        want to hear.

21

# LEAVING NAZARETH

How long did it take,
   Master,
before it was clear
   that the hour had come
to fulfil the thirty quiet years
   of Galilee
   and Nazareth?
So putting away the tools,
telling a final story to the children,
bidding farewell to mother and home,
then out on the road
   to the world.
No place to rest your head
   under the tree where
      the birds had their nest
near the lair of the fox
   and its cubs
under the open sky,
loving the whole creation,
hailing every man,
no fixed home
   but at home
      everywhere.
How long did it take
   for the call to come?
How long to obey it?
   How long for me?

# STANDING WITH MEN

Mark 1.9-11

O my Lord,
the Father's voice
and the inflow of Spirit
confirmed the faith
    that called you out of Nazareth.

Let me, like you,
seeking the Father's will,
responding in faith,
    receive the sonship
    and the power.

O my Lord,
you stood with men,
one of them
in their sins, their penitences
      and their hopes.

Let me be as human as you,
not condemning,
praying your last prayer
at my beginning:
    'They know not what they do.'

Yet I have so much sin
that you must take away,
O Lamb of God, for me
before I can stand
    with you for others.

23

c

# IN THE WILDERNESS
Mark 1.12

Forty days
in the harsh desert
alone with the wild creatures,
in caves
and under the stars
    to discover the Father's will,
    to learn how to use
        the Spirit's power,
    to recognize the subtle defection,
    the desire for miracle and fame,
    the short-cut to success,
    the cunning compromise,
    the means that would defeat the end.
What then, O Father,
    is the truth, the will, the way?
Only the way of love
    of service,
    of suffering.
Already a cross
    at the end of the road,
And beyond that?
    Only you, O Father,
    waiting to welcome
        your beloved Son
    and the twelve legions of angels
    and all the saints of heaven and earth,
        O dear my Lord.

# ONLY THE SHADOW

Mark 1.12

The Spirit drove him
    to commune with God.
The initiative was his,
    not of the evil one,
To discover the purpose
    and decide the way.
Evil is secondary,
    an intruder, a dark shadow, an attacker
        who seeks to deflect,
        corrupting the means,
        shaping the end.
    Yet for the moment
        occupying the stage,
        compelling the attention
        until a word betrays
        the evil intent
        and the eye of faith
            pierces the disguise
        and sees the good Spirit
            waiting in the wings.
Get thee behind me, Satan!
    Come, Holy Spirit,
        Come!

25

# GUEST PREACHER

Luke 4.16-21

O Christ my Lord,
Bibles and books were not so easily available
    to you as to me,
And I marvel at your choice
    of this text
    to be the mainspring of your ministry:
To bring good news to the poor —
    there are so many poor today,
To bind up the broken hearted —
    O Lord, there is still so much grief,
To bring release to the prisoners —
    still so many prisons of fear, despair and sin
    as well as political and judicial,
To usher in the year of jubilee
    when all debts shall be cancelled,
    all pledges restored,
    all slaves freed.
I marvel too, my Lord,
    at the point where you stopped,
    no mention of divine vengeance,
Only good news, Godspell.
O Lord, let the Church
    listen to the Nazareth sermon,
    be the Nazareth sermon,
Fulfilling before the world
    the programme of gospel
    which you announced.

# RECRUITING

Luke 6.12-16

O Lord,
   how long did you know them
   before you asked them
      to join in your mission to men?
Did you look into their faces,
   see into their souls,
   draw out their thoughts
      and hopes and fears?
In that night of prayer
   what did you pray?
You needed twelve
   for the renewal of Israel,
   for its extension
      to all mankind
      in every age.
They were to catch men
   as you caught them,
      to tell good news,
      to spread love,
Until in turn I am caught
   and must live
   within your circle
      of missioning love.

# DOCTOR'S SURGERY

Matthew 9.12

'Those who are well
   have no need of a physician,
   but those who are sick.'
O Jesus, my Lord,
   at Matthew's farewell party
   did you realize his need
   for spiritual help and cure?
You can do so much for those
   who know their own need
   of change within their souls.
Prescribe for me, my Lord,
   for I want to be
   whole
      and holy,
   to be healed
   and then to heal
      with you.

# AN AWFUL MISTAKE?

Mark 14.17-21   Matthew 27.3-5

Lord, when you chose Judas
    You must have hoped in him
    although you knew
    he was not heartwhole.
I cannot believe
    that it was sheer treachery
    but some awful mistake
    to force your hand
    in tragic self-will.
Yet you took it up
    into your texture of life,
    into the seamless robe
    of the Father's purpose.
Lord, was he too in your mind
    when you made excuse
    from the cross?
Did you seek him out
    in the place of the dead
    with the other two?
O Christ, I ask with the others,
    Is it I? Is it I?
    Can it be me?
For I do not want to betray you
    Knowingly or unknowingly.
Grant that I may be heartwhole
    in my loyalty,
    even though, like the others,

I am weak,
trembling
and confused,
but still your disciple.

# MY SPHERE AND YOURS
Luke 7.1-10

'In my own sphere
   I have authority,
   my officers and men obey,
   my servant is quick
   to carry out my commands,
   anticipate my wishes.
You in your sphere
   have authority
   in the dimension of the spiritual
   over the spirits of men,
   over health and life and death;
   Say the word only.'
Because your realm is the spiritual
   you do not need to go or come,
   the message and power of your spirit
   are enough.
Distance and time do not operate
   in your sphere,
   you are always
   immediate and present,
   there and here.
You bring courage
   to the doubting spirit
   and meaning
   to the troubled mind
   and calm to the fevered brow.

The evil spirits
   and the divided spirits,
   the demonic forces
   from without or within
   cry out,
For they know
   that their reign is over,
   a greater power has come,
   the finger of God in command
   is stronger than the pointing
   finger of accusation, evil, terror, malice
   and magic.
You by the finger of God
   heal men's spirits, minds and bodies
   making them whole,
   giving them love,
   bringing them grace.
In you the Kingdom of God
   has drawn near.
Blessed are you, O Lord,
   and blessed is your Kingdom
      for ever.

# AT THE DINNER
Luke 14. 7-11

Here I am
   in the lowest room
   as the Master commanded,
waiting for him to come
   and call me to the high table
   with the great ones of the earth
   and heaven.
He is long in coming,
   the dinner is nearly finished,
   and still I am here
   in the lowest room
   with the unimportant men.
I must attract his attention,
   talk more loudly,
   tell a witty story
   so that all look this way
   at the sound of the laughter.
Oh! he is rising from his place
   and coming my way,
   soon the promised promotion
   and honour before all
   as he arms me to his table.
No? he sits down here
   at the lowest table
   with these unimportant ones
   as gracious to them as to me.
Is this all I get
   for continuing duty,

33

for years of public service,
for accepted humility?
I will stay no longer,
  I will make some excuse
  and take my leave
  away from those eyes
  that disturb my peace,
  leave me uneasy,
  as if he knew
  . . . as if he knew
  the man I am
  behind my mask
  of humility.

# THE SEED IS THE WORD
Luke 8.11

In nature the seed
    has the germ of life within it,
    the power of germination,
    the thin blade
    pierces through the earth
    and becomes a plant,
    a bush, a tree.
So within the human spirit
    you sow a word
    which will lie hidden
    and then burst into life,
    bearing fruit in maturity,
    character and action.
The order of growth
    in the harvest of spirit
    is the same as in nature
    thirty-, sixty-, a hundred-fold.
All I have to do
    is to hold it
    in the dark of my spirit
    in inner warmth;
    your word like a seed
    does the rest.
My spirit must lie open
    to your Spirit
    like the earth
    to the seasons of the year.

At the right moment
the word will germinate,
push down its roots,
push up its leaves,
its flower,
its fruit
and become the full expression
of the seed you gave,
O divine Sower.

# WAITING FOR JESUS
Luke 8.40

There had always been
   an unconscious need
   of someone like him
who would understand
   and not condemn,
who would always excuse —
   'they know not what they do' —
who would see them
   as sheep not having a shepherd
   but needing a shepherd,
who would see them
   not only as they are
   but as they might become
   in his company,
who would encourage each
   in his own task,
   in his own difficulties,
   in all his opportunities,
and having found him
   they did not want to lose him,
   and when he withdrew for a time
   they missed him.
Of course they welcomed him
   for they had always been waiting
   for someone like him
And now he had come
   so they pressed around him,
   hung on his words,

felt his forgiveness
and the stir of new hope.
When we have found him
    all we have to do
    is to stay with him,
    following wherever he leads,
    making him welcome
    eternally.
Sometimes he seems elsewhere,
    away or hidden
    or perhaps only ahead.
    Desire will draw him back;
    he will return,
    smiling his welcome
    in response to ours.

# NO TROUBLE TO HIM

Luke 8.49

'Your daughter is dead:
do not trouble the Master any more.'

There is nothing more to be done,
    nothing that anyone can do
    except to bury the dead.

An hour earlier
    it might have been of some use,
    but now it is too late,
    don't bother the Master.

The Master's reply —
    Do not fear; only believe
    all shall be well;
    there is no death,
    only sleep,
    falling asleep here — waking there,
    still within reach of the Master's voice.

The Master spans both worlds,
    this and that,
    can hear the messages we send
    and speak them on the other side,
    take the love of our hearts
    and warm theirs.

To each one who crosses the border
    He says,
        Little one, rise.
Faith restores each little one to her parents.

So trouble the Master —
    trust in his over-arching care
    radio-ing messages of love
    through him.

Don't neglect the gift
    of a go-between Lord,
    don't fail those ahead
    by neglectful forgetfulness.

She is not dead, she slept
    and woke, and still
    is within sound of his voice.

It is no trouble to the Master
    for he too has slept that sleep
    and awakened.

## 'LOOSE ME, LORD!'
John 11.43-4


O Lord,
   I am Lazarus
   bound with the grave clothes
   of habits and fears,
   struggling towards the light
   through the opening
   of the rolled away stone,
   answering thy command —
      'Lazarus, come forth!'
   awaiting the second command —
      'Loose him and let him go.'
   Loose me from habits and fears,
   the dead hand of the past,
   into new freedom, new life,
   ready to obey
   thy further commands.

# TO JESUS

Colossians 1.15    John 1.18

If I must have an image
you are the best of all,
for you don't let me stay with you
but point me to the Father,
take me to Him,
    Your Father and mine,
    Your God and mine.

Most satisfying Image,
so good that anyone
staying with you
might be tempted
to stay with you
and not go on with you
    to the Father.

The image of the invisible God,
Human face of the divine light,
Truth in a person,
The Way in a life,
Love in death and beyond
    and all from God.

Lord, let me take you as model,
reproduce the likeness,
receive you in person
in the depths of my being,
for you are the Everliving One,
Everpresent with the Father
in glory, in the imaging universe,
in the human soul,
in time and in eternity.

# HE WILLING TO JUSTIFY HIMSELF

Luke 10.29

O Lord,
    I am like him
    wanting to justify,
    wanting to be right,
    wanting to make excuses.

Let me
    never measure myself
    by myself or by others
    but only by thee,
    by thy perfection.

Let me
    accept myself,
    my fallibility,
    my self-regarding,
    my need of wisdom
    and grace.

Then, Lord
    referring everything to thee,
    seeking thy will,
    relying on thy grace,

Let me
    grow in maturity
    towards the goal
    of likeness to thy Son,
    justified only by him.

# A CASTAWAY?

1 Corinthians 9.27

Lest I myself should be
    a castaway:

Talking about the good news
    and never believing it,
    accepting it,
    enjoying it,

Only saying prayers
    and taking services
    and never worshipping,
    seldom praying,

For ever talking about the Lord
    and never hearing Him
    or knowing Him
    in living touch,

Castaway
    upon my own little island,
    starved of the company
    of my fellow-men.

O cast me not away
    from thy presence
    nor take thy Holy Spirit
    from me.

# LATE BIRTH

John 3.4


'How can a man be born
    when he is old?'
His character is formed,
his habits fixed,
people think they know him,
    can predict
    what attitude he will take,
    what he will say.
To begin again,
become a new person:
what will his family say,
what will his friends think?
At my age, I cannot change,
I'm too old, too far gone,
I've tried everything
    and it hasn't worked —
As impossible as to return
    to the womb.
Can the Kingdom of God
    be worth all this travail?
From the house-top in Jerusalem
    under cover of the night
    with the gentle breath of the wind
comes the quiet insistent voice
    of this man
    to whom I feel strangely drawn;
I must be born again,
    he says.

Not yet, not tonight —
But I can never forget,
    for He has sown a seed,
    a soul is conceived
    but not yet born again,
    for 'not yet' is promise
        of a birth ahead.
O Lord, how wise you were,
    how perceptive,
    how penetrating.

# STILL TO BE PRAYED

John 16.24


Take no notice, Lord, of my unloving prayers,
    my selfish prayers,
    my imperfect prayers,
except to note that I am speaking to you
    and if I listen, you will answer
    and chide me gently
    and cleanse the heart
that wants to talk with you but sometimes asks
    short-sighted prayers,
    selfish prayers,
    immature prayers.
Teach me to pray the prayers
that you would pray,
the prayers that you are already
working to answer,
    O dear Lord.

# GREATLY BELOVED
Daniel 9.23

Enlarge my heart
   to the dimensions of your heart,
   O Limitless Love.
Let nothing be thought
   common or unclean
   which thou hast cleansed.
Let no one be thought
   too exalted, so that
   I only respect
   but do not love.
Let nobody be regarded
   as too humble, so that
   I patronize or despise.
Let none be thought
   as of little value
   and written off,
For each is dear to thee
   with his own potential
   and his own hope
   and his own heartbreak.
Let me say to each with thee,
   'O man greatly beloved'
   infinitely and eternally
   dear to thee
O Lord Love,
   enlarge my heart
   to the dimension
   of thine.

49

# HOW TO LOVE

1 John 4.19

O Lord, you teach me
    that there is only one cure
    for hatred,
    namely love.
But what if I have no love?
'Then, my child,
    you must learn to love.'
Lord, how do I begin?
'By accepting love,
    my love, the Father's love.
    When you accept love
    you begin to love in return.
'Don't look so sceptical —
    your mother loved you
    before you were born
    and when you were
    a helpless scrap of humanity;
'Your father loved you
    with protective, providing love.
'You felt secure,
    wanted, valued, care-free
    because of their love.
'Let your heavenly Father love you,
    my Father and yours,
    and you will love in return.
'Our love, the Father's and mine,
    must grow in you,
    must move outward

to all other children of his.
'And if it is true love,
   selfless and undemanding,
   it will dissolve the other's hatred,
   sweeten his bitterness,
   disarm his aggressiveness,
   heal his pain
   and beget love in return.'
How long will it take, my Lord?
'It depends on you, my child,
   how deeply you have felt my love
   and responded.
'It cannot fail, because it was love
   which created the universe,
   begat man in love
   and kept the welcoming arms outstretched
   even on a cross.
'Love, my child,
   because you are so greatly,
   so eternally loved.'

# THE LAST FARTHING

Matthew 5.26

Lord,
   I have not much to offer
   but let me give it all,
Let me pay the uttermost farthing
   keeping nothing back,
   giving without grudging the cost,
   so eager and willing
   that I do not even count the cost,
   knowing that the divine treasury
   is inexhaustible,
   always open to my need,
   so that there is no last farthing,
     O my God.
When I have given my last farthing
   you give me ten more,
   or five,
   or even just one more
   to invest for you
   and come again for more.

# PRESUMPTUOUS?

John 5.24—5

Would it be presumptuous, Lord,
   to hope or even believe
   that as you shared our humanity
   and we begin to share
   the humanity you transformed
   the dead too may hear our voice
   as they heard yours?

You called Lazarus by name,
   you spoke to the widow's son at Nain
   and the little daughter
   of the president of the synagogue
   and all three heard
   and came at your call,
   their first returning sight
      your smiling face.

The little girl
   only a minute or two away,
   the young man
   hours on, to the graveyard,
   Lazarus four days gone,
   Moses and Elijah
      centuries away in time.

Lord, could I call
   the name of my parted loved one,

perhaps repeating it many a time
for my silence might have sent him
    out of spiritual earshot.

My lack of faith
    might have dimmed my spiritual eye
    to see beyond the horizon
    over which he has passed,
    for death is only an horizon
    and an horizon
        but the limit of our sight.

Could I speak each day
    feeling him still present
    tell him of continuing love
    receive the assurance
    that his love too endures
    in thee and through thee
    in the milieu
        of the Father's omnipresence?

Lord, would it be presumptuous
    to hope that my dead hear my voice
    as the three in Caparnaum, Nain and Bethany
    heard your dear voice?
    Lord, knowing something of you
    and your Father and mine
        I will presume!

# MAKING GOD OUR FATHER

Matthew 5.48

O God, You tell me
   that You are my Father.
Let me be truly and fully
   Your son.
Let me be constantly
in glad, natural, filial relationship
   with You.
Let me understand Your purpose,
   want nothing but Your ways of working
      and Your values of living,
   being what You want me to be,
   doing what You want done,
   saying the thoughts which come from You.
Let me be a son, a true son, a beloved son,
   an obedient son, a mature son
   as was Jesus, Your perfect and beloved son
      through whom I came to You
      and call You Abba — Father,
      Father — dear Father.

# FATHER AND SONS

John 20.17


LET GOD
   be Father
   speak
   liberate me from my prisons
   direct my path
   infuse me with His grace and love.

LET ME
   be son
   listen
   walk out of my prisons through opened doors
   follow his guidance
   open up my being to His grace and love,

   Study and imitate
   the perfect sonship
   of Jesus Christ
   the universal brother
   of all other sons.

# YOUNGER BROTHERS
Romans 8.29


O Christ,
  You are representative Son
  and representative brother.
If I am truly a son
I must be fully a brother
  and everyone be brother or sister to me.
As first brother you want mutual love
  within the family of God
  and the family of man.
Let me have a care for everyone,
  a desire to know each one,
  an interest in what each wants to be,
  a warmness of heart,
  a welcome of eye, a smile of pleasure
  in recognizing another son
  or daughter of the Father
  from whose heart you came
  and to whose heart you would lead us,
    O first-born Son and Universal Brother.

# RECOGNIZING FAITH

Matthew 8.10

'I have not found such great faith,
no, not in Israel.'

You knew the meaning of faith,
   O my Lord.
For you had such faith
   in the Father;
You knew the men of faith
   in Israel's Bible
   and men of faith in your own day
   and strugglers for faith.
I know, O Lord,
   God's gift of faith is not reserved
   for men in Israel only.
Your Church, O Lord,
   has no monopoly of faith;
It is a gift of God
   to every man.
Grant
that I may recognize it
   in other men
and know that we are
   brothers in faith
in Israel, in the Church
   or outside,
    but all of us
      in the community of faith.

# MEN ON THE MOUNTAIN

Mark 9.4

Night on the mountain-top,
   Tabor or Hermon,
   it matters little,
Above the sleeping countryside
   the villages and fields and people
   under the stars
   in communion with the Father
With the bright moon
   revealing the joy
   on the Master's face
   with a halo
      of unearthly beauty
   and a sense of heavenly presence
   as if advised
      by the great ones
      from the past.
Moses with memories of Sinai,
   the giving of the divine law,
   the mountain of covenant
   commands for the two great duties
      to God and to man
   the making of a God-ruled nation,
   a nation of priests to the world
   in vocation if never yet in fact.

Moses on another mountain
    viewing the land of hope
        and promise,
    the homeland of Abraham,
        willing to offer a son
    but prevented by a God
        who will himself
        provide a Lamb
        in his own time.
Elijah with the memory
    of Carmel's false gods
    and the triumph of Yahweh
    and the slaughter
    tragically conceived as divine will.
Elijah at Horeb
    learning a new lesson —
        Not in earthquake
        wind
        fire
But in the still small voice
    spoken within the heart
    in gentleness and love,
    not thundering from fire and smoke,
Conferring with two forerunners,
    fulfiller of both,
    by a new and better way
    the priest himself
    becoming the sacrifice.

Three others on the mountain
   watching in wonder and awe
   and hearing another
      still small voice:
   'This is my beloved Son,
      hear him, obey him, follow him
      wherever he leads.'
At the foot of the mountain
   men with their griefs and sins
   which can only be healed
   by those who have been
   on the mountain-top
      with the transfigured Lord.

# HOUR OF GLORY

John 17.1


Lord, you were not only tempted
for forty days down by Jordan
but constantly all through
   your ministry

Not to obvious blatant sins
but to subtler defections
from the Father's will;
to cunning compromises
which would defeat
   the Father's purpose.

And as the last days drew near
the evil efforts were redoubled,
for the spirit of evil knew
that the last and fiercest strife
   was close at hand.

The Greeks who wanted to greet you —
did their coming suggest
a wider mission
where men would listen
   and welcome you?

You saw the evasion of the cross
in their innocent request
and knew that without the death of the seed
   there would be no harvest in nature.

So without your own sacrifice
there would be no harvest of souls.
Only uttermost love
loving in death
    could avail.

In the garden of olives
across the valley
you wrestled with the doubt
that death could be
    the Father's will.

Agony of soul and sweat of blood
before the issue was decided;
then stepping forth
calm and unafraid
you offered your hands
    for the handcuffs.

Before Pilate you could have
pleaded your case
against your accusers —
your only appeal
to the kingdom of truth.

In the fiercest moments of pain
with piercing nails
and the dragging body
and the mocking cry:
    *Come down from the cross*
    *and we will believe.*

Could you have come down
or was it love that held you there?
or the full humanity
that holds others
    to their crosses?

You stayed on the Cross
bleeding, powerless,
uttering words of love
    to God and men.

Only one temptation more,
most subtle and shattering,
a blanket of darkness
and whispering doubt:
    *What if God too*
    *has forsaken you?*

Here comes the final test of faith,
here the last claim of love,
here the fiercest attack of evil:
    *What if God has forsaken you?*

O Christ, my Lord, I stand
obedient with you
at the foot of your cross
in darkness with you,
waiting and listening;
my faith at stake
    with yours.

Until at last comes a great cry
of pain and faith:
    'My God! My God!

*lama sabachthani,*
Why, why am I forsaken?'
Yet still 'My God! My God!'

The strife is o'er,
the battle done,
the last temptation met;
faith complete,
the task finished,
evil defeated,
love triumphant:
>   *Father,*
>   *into thy hands*
>   *I commend my spirit —*
>   *the rest lies with you,*
>   *Abba, Father,*
>       *Father, dear Father.*

Surely, here by the cross
with the limp body
there must have sounded
the voice from heaven
>   once more:
>       'This is my beloved Son
>       Son in call,
>       Son in obedience,
>       Son in love,
>       Son in death
>       and in triumphant life:
>       *My Son, my own dear Son,*
>       *Jesus of Nazareth,*
>       *My Son! My Son!'*

65

# 'DO NOT HOLD ME'
John 20.17

Don't hold me to the past;
a new era has dawned,
a new dimension added
   to life itself.

Between now and then
there stands a cross,
for six long hours
a cross of pain
but now an empty cross
and an empty tomb.

Obedience unto death
is release from death,
not the end of the obeying spirit
but its universal presence.

No longer nailed to a cross,
confined to one fixed place,
limited to the moment of time,

But omnipresent
and immediate,
quick to move
with the speed of light,
with the speed of thought
and swifter still
with the speed of love
and the power of God.

66

# TELLING OTHERS

Luke 8.39

Not as missionary technique
    but in simple gratitude,
    realizing what I would have been
        without God's work for me;
Not closing the book
    of God's action on me,
    rooted only in the past,
    even of some significant act
    which can be dated,
    which made all the difference
        to my life;
But grateful for that act
    and opening up more of my being
    to his continuing grace,
    greater, deeper action
    calling out greater, deeper
        gratitude;
Not in boastful pride
    but in humble thanksgiving,
    expecting his continuing grace
    in deeper, humbler love
        and self-forgetfulness.
But what if I have not
    allowed God to do for me
    what He knows I need,
    making me
        what He wants me to be?

67

New life can begin now,
   at any moment
   in any year of age;
   all I have to ask is —
   'Lord, what do you want me to do?
   What kind of man
   do you want me to be?
   Where do I start?'
I know you will answer,
   speak plainly, piercingly,
   right to the heart —
   heal me, Lord,
   remake me
   so that my life may show
   without the need of words
   what you have done for me.

# A PERSONAL QUESTION

John 21.15


Lovest thou me?
   O Christ, my dear
   O Christ, dear man
   O Christ, dear Lord
Thou knowest that I love thee.

In spite of faithlessness
   failure, denial
There is none other to whom I can go.

I love thee, my Lord
   because thou hast first loved me.
My love is but response to thine.

You bid me feed thy sheep
   tend thy little ones
   seek thy lost ones
   lost, stolen or strayed
   with no one to guide them,
   the other ones
   not of thy fold
In different folds
   but all one flock
   under one shepherd
Dear Lord, thou knowest
   that I love thee
   and them.

# BLESSED WITHOUT SEEING

John 20.29

Lord, I know the eye of faith
   sees farther
   than the physical eye,
For with the eye of faith
   we can see
   the evidence of things not seen;
We can see behind the scenes,
   beyond the horizon,
   into the spiritual,
   into the eternal;
We can see Love at work
   beyond the evidence
   of the senses.
Lord, grant that I may value
   the eye of faith
   equally with the eyes
   of the body,
Seeing behind the veil of happenings
   into the realm
   of meaning and purpose
For the real world is the spiritual,
   the eternal,
   the creative, the redemptive.
O let me have the blessing
   promised by thee,
   the sight that sees through
To see thee who art invisible
   and thine Everliving Christ

        reigning with thee,
        working with thee;
And seeing thee at work
        know that at the end
        the material shall be transformed
        into the spiritual;

And all shall be well,
All manner of thing shall be well.

# THROUGH JESUS CHRIST

Matthew 27.51


Can Jesus be a barrier to God?
    Do I stop at him
    and not go on to the Father
    from whom he came?

Do I not see the centrality of God
    to him,
    the priority of God,
    the allness of God?

Must I not pass through him
    to the God from whom he came,
    and having passed beyond him
        as I think or fear
    find him there in the heart of the Father?

But those who stay with him
    are blest
    in having reached as far,
for the Everliving One
    will one day lead them, take them
        to the heart of the Eternal Father.

# THE ROUND WORLD

Psalm 93.2 (Book of Common Prayer)


I'm glad that the world is round,
    for however far I go
    I shall come back home again;
    I shall not fall off
        into nothingness.
Journeying alone maybe,
    yet sooner or later
    I shall meet another soul,
    our meridians crossing.
Men can take off
    from any point
    for other spheres
    and return to this.
The Spirit of God
    reaches from one end
    to the other,
    around and return.
Whither shall I go, then,
    from thy presence,
    be deaf to thy voice,
    escape from thy love?
The morning stars still shout
    with ever-deepening joy,
    the music of the spheres
    still sings
    around the world
    and through the planets
        of endless space.

# UNEXPECTED TREASURE

Psalm 119.162

'I am as glad of thy Word
    as one that findeth great spoils.'
    As a man stumbling on buried treasure in a field,
        selling all he has to buy that field;
    As a man who knows all about pearls,
        coming across one of priceless beauty
        so perfect that he cannot be happy
        until he possesses it,
        so sells all that he has
        and with eager joy
        buys that pearl;
    As a young man with great possessions
        desiring the deep quality of life
        at last ready to give away all that he has
        to enter the Kingdom of the Spirit
        and make it the greatest
            of his possessions,
            his only treasure;
O God, I am glad, unspeakably glad
    for thy Word and thy Kingdom.

74

# EVERYDAY SAINTS

Revelation 7.9

A great crowd
   that no man can number
   out of every race and tongue,
simple souls who want to be
   what you want them to be
and to do
   what you want done
and to bear
   all that is your will,
living by the truth they know,
   eager for more,
forgetting themselves
   but never forgetting you,
perfect simplicity
   with regard to themselves,
perfect contentment
   with all that comes their way,
perfect peace of mind
   in utter self-forgetfulness,
realizing only
   the greatness
   and goodness,
   the all-ness
   of you,
      O King of saints.

# DARE TO BE GAMALIEL!
Acts 5.33—9


'If this plan be only of men
   it will fail,
but if it be of God
   nothing can defeat it.
You might be found
   opposing God.'

Men arise
giving themselves out
to be somebody,
a flash in the plan,
headline for a day,
even an interview
   on radio or TV;

A new slogan
publicized at great expense,
finally recognized
as only a slogan,
not speaking to reality,
not from God.

If it be of God
   beware, for nothing can stop it,
   only hinder or delay,
yet your acceptance
   can advance its purpose,
   hasten its blessing.

Primal man
feeling a presence
by the spring,
in the forest,
by the banyan tree,
fearing the spirits,
not yet seeing
    Holy Spirit.

In Israel
Abraham, father of faith,
patriarchs, prophets, kings, saints
experiencing God,
accepting His Law,
continuing faith
    down to today.

Through human history
prophets have arisen,
some consciously speaking from God,
some in devotion to truth
and concern for men,
not knowing the source
    of their message.

Ikhanaton,
lonely king of Egypt,
finding the Creator a century before Moses
    behind the sun,
and the Creator's power
    in nature's workings.

The Buddha
with universal compassion

finding the escape
   from suffering
in denying desire,
in following the eightfold
   path of virtue.

Zoroaster,
peer with Israel's prophets
seeing history and human life
   as a battlefield
   between good and evil,
   truth and the lie.

The Bhagavad Gita,
quintessence of India's spirituality
seeking the One behind the many,
believing divine incarnation
leading from the unreal to the real,
from darkness to light,
from death to immortality.

Muhammad
in Abrahamic imitation
calling his people
   from idols and superstition
   to the worship of God,
Lord of the Worlds,
the Compassionate One.

Each with a gospel
   to his own people
at a moment when
   human need was met
by divine grace
   through human agents.

O Christ, my Lord,
if any or all of these
  brought such truth and joy
  as you have brought to me
  what inexhaustible riches
  is the world's heritage,

Let me welcome
  and listen to the message of each,
see how it relates
  to what I already have,
enlarging my vision
  of God at work;

See thee as Divine Word
inspiring what is true,
correcting what is mistaken,
begetting love,
strengthening goodness,
drawing all forward
  to the embrace
  of the Father's love.

O Christ, my Lord,
let me be as wise and open
  to all seekers of truth,
  all practitioners of love,
  all livers of virtue
as Gamaliel
  expecting to find
  the Father at work.

# RABIA

Rabia was a Muslim woman saint
who lived first in Basrah and then
in Jerusalem around 800 A.D.


Lord, there was a woman in Jerusalem
    whom I want to meet
    in Paradise
to thank her for her insights
    and her prayers,
    prayed like mine
        in Jerusalem,
who feared neither hell
    nor desired any heaven
    but to know
    thy eternal beauty,
who for years was a slave
    cruelly treated
    but free in spirit
    wanting only thy will.


More than a thousand years
    between Rabia and me, O Lord,
        in Jerusalem —
Only you can span
    those long years,
        O Everliving One;
Only you can bridge
    this world and the next,
    and both are hers and mine
        in you.

So, dear Lord,
    give her my gratitude
    for what she was
    and how she prayed
        in Jerusalem.

## 'BEHOLD THE LAMB OF GOD
## WHO TAKES AWAY
## THE SIN OF THE WORLD'

John 1.29

The sins of the world,
   such dreadful sins,
   not just the personal sins
   but the solidarity of sin,
   greater than the total
     of individual sins,
   nuclear evil in endless fission,
     O Lamb of God.

The sin of racial pride
   that sees not the faith
     that all men are divinely made
   nor the riches of pigment
     in portrait faces,
   the same psychology
   and religious search,
   that each is the sibling
     for whom Christ died.

The burgeoning greed
   that never heeds the need of others
   involved in a merciless system,
   looking only at profit and dividend,
   the lust of possessions
     that cannot accompany us
     at our last migration:

Take away these sins,
    O Lamb of God.

The hatred that must destroy
    if self-will is crossed
    or frustration too impatient
    no matter who is hurt,
       innocent or guilty,
    coming not to fulfil or change
       but to destroy:
Take away this sin,
    O Lamb of God

The massive sin of war,
    millions of lives impersonally destroyed,
    trillions of pounds wasted
    on weapons, bombs,
    truth enslaved,
    the hungry still unfed,
    grief stalking unnumbered homes:
Weep over us,
    O Lamb of God.

The sin of the world,
    alienation from thee,
    not just weakness
    but evil intention,
    organized and unrestrained
    with its own momentum
    leading to death:
O Lamb of God,
    take away this sin.

Begin with me,
O Lamb of God,
   forgive my sins,
   cleanse my heart,
   disarm my will
   and let me fight
   only with truth, love and righteousness
   with thy cross of love
   incised upon my heart,
      O Lamb of God.